HOW TO KNOW WHICH ANGEL TO CALL UPON

88 Angel Attributes
Listed Alphabetically

Including
Angel Affirmations

CREATED BY JO DANCE
WWW.JODANCE.CO.UK

Contents

Introduction	1
How to use this book	3
Frequently asked questions	5
Gaining a higher perspective	8
Index of attributes and associated angels	9
About the author	189

Introduction

Something often asked by those who are drawn to connect with angels is 'how do I know which angel to call upon?'

The good news is that you don't need to call upon angels by their specific names for them to help you.

Instead, you can simply say (either out loud or silently to yourself) 'thank you angels for helping me with...'

Trust and know your request has been received, and let any attachment to the outcome go.

The relevant angel(s) will respond accordingly.

You may not be consciously aware of the angelic assistance being received, however - simply trust and know all requests are received and responded to in relation to the highest purpose of all, and divine timing.

If you would rather call in angels specifically by their name, based on what they are known for helping with, this book can assist you.

How to use this book

This book can be used in different ways:

Search by attribute
Attributes are listed alphabetically with the relevant angel to call upon. Simply search for the attribute in the index, then turn to the relevant page.

Ask and be guided
Whether you have a particular request in mind or not, you may suddenly feel inspired to pick up this book and discover what the angels want you to know.

In this case, you might like to simply hold the book to your heart for a few moments, focus on your breath, and intend to connect with the angels. When you feel guided to do so, open the book.

The relevant angel for you in that moment will be revealed (even if this doesn't make sense to you on a conscious level).

Angel affirmations
There is an angel affirmation with each attribute, so you can begin to align with the vibration of your request having already been received and responded to.

This in itself starts to create a positive shift.

The affirmations were channelled at the time of creating this book, with the intention of them holding the frequency of the relevant attributes to assist with alignment, and connection to the relevant angels.

If there is part of an affirmation that doesn't resonate with you, simply change this so it does.

You can easily make each affirmation work for you.

Frequently asked questions

'How many times should I make my request, and if I ask more than once, will the response be more powerful?'

You only need to express your request or affirmation once for it to be received. The response will not be more powerful if you keep asking.

What's more important is how you feel when you are making your request.

Is this coming from need or fear, or from a place of trusting all is as it's meant to be, without attachment to a specific outcome manifesting how and when you think it should?

We attract in alignment with our vibration, therefore the latter is definitely preferable.

I know this can sometimes be easier said than done - especially in relation to challenges we are personally experiencing, or other challenges we are aware of.

However, the more you practice aligning with the affirmations knowing they have been responded to, the more likely you are to notice how your energy shifts from a feeling of fear to a feeling of calm and peace.

This energy benefits all.

Frequently asked questions

'Do I need to be qualified to work with angels and have experienced attunements for them to respond to me?'

No. Angels are here to help everyone. They just need permission to do so.

Your intention when reading the affirmations in this book (or simply thanking the angels for their help) is all the permission they need to respond.

Attending workshops, training, and experiencing attunements can deepen your connection with angels, but this is a personal choice.

Frequently asked questions

'Why don't I always see evidence of my requests having been received and responded to?'

When you ask, it IS given. However, this won't necessarily be in the way you are expecting, or when you would like it to be.

Allow yourself to be open to noticing evidence of your positive shift in vibration - opposed to looking for evidence how you think your request should manifest.

Gaining a higher perspective

We all experience challenges as we go through life.

The things we overcome help us to evolve and grow, in many ways, and on many levels.

Connecting with angels to align with their love and light can lift our vibration, and helps us to perceive things from a higher perspective.

This benefits us personally, and also benefits others, as our energy is contagious.

Index of attributes and associated angels

Abundance - Archangel Raphael - 12
Addictions (Clearing) - Archangel Tzaphkiel - 14
Akashic Records - Archangel Metatron - 16
All is Well - Archangel Jeremiel - 18
Angelic Reiki - Archangel Metatron - 20
Animal Kingdom - Archangel Ariel - 22
Argument Resolution - Archangel Raguel - 24
Beauty in Ourselves - Archangel Haniel - 26
Career - Archangel Chamuel - 28
Cleansing & Clearing - Archangel Michael - 30
Communication - Archangel Gabriel - 32
Compassion - Archangel Zadkiel - 34
Conception/Pregnancy/Birth - Archangel Gabriel - 36
Cord Cutting - Archangel Michael - 38
Courage - Archangel Michael - 40
Creativity - Archangel Gabriel - 42
Death/Dying/Grieving - Archangel Azrael - 44
Decision Making - Archangel Jeremiel - 46
Direction - Archangel Michael - 48
Divine Guidance - Archangel Jeremiel - 50
Dreams & Visions - Archangel Jeremiel - 52
Empowerment - Archangel Raguel - 54
Energy Levels - Archangel Michael - 56
Eyesight - Archangel Raphael - 58
Follow Healing Path - Archangel Raphael - 60
Follow Heart - Archangel Michael - 62
Forgivness - Archangel Zadkiel - 64
Fresh Start - Archangel Raphael - 66
Good Weather - Archangel Uriel - 68

Grace - Archangel Haniel - 70
Harmony - Archangel Raguel - 72
Healing - Archangel Raphael - 74
Healing Modality Support - Archangel Raphael - 76
Healthy Habits - Archangel Tzaphkiel - 78
Higher Realm Connection - Archangel Tzaphkiel - 80
Home - Archangel Jophiel - 82
Inner Guidance - Archangel Jophiel - 84
Intellect - Archangel Uriel - 86
Intuition - Archangels Jeremiel & Tzaphkiel - 88
Intuitive Skills - Archangel Haniel - 90
Kindness - Archangel Zadkiel - 92
Knowledge - Archangel Uriel - 94
Law of Attraction - Archangel Jophiel - 96
Letting Go - Archangel Michael - 98
Life Purpose - Archangel Chamuel - 100
Life Review - Archangel Jeremiel - 102
Loss - Archangel Azrael - 104
Lost Items - Archangel Chamuel - 106
Love - Archangel Chamuel - 108
Loving Relationships - Archangel Chamuel - 110
Manifestation - Archangels Ariel & Raziel - 112
Manifesting Desires - Archangel Jophiel - 114
Mediation - Archangel Raguel - 116
Meditation - Archangel Tzaphkiel - 118
Memory Function/Recall - Archangel Zadkiel - 120
Moon Energies - Archangel Haniel - 122
Motivation - Archangel Michael - 124
Music - Archangel Sandalphon - 126
Natural Disasters - Archangel Uriel - 128
Nature - Archangel Ariel - 130
Negative Thoughts - Archangel Tzaphkiel - 132

Parenting - Archangel Gabriel - 134
Patience - Archangel Jophiel - 136
Peace - Archangel Uriel - 138
Persistence with Pursuits - Archangel Jophiel - 140
Positive Thoughts - Archangel Jophiel - 142
Practical Solutions - Archangel Uriel - 144
Prayer Delivery - Archangel Sandalphon - 146
Problem Solving - Archangels Metatron & Uriel - 148
Protection - Archangel Michael - 150
Psychic Abilities - Archangels Haniel & Raziel - 152
Record Keeping - Archangel Metatron - 154
Rest - Archangel Gabriel - 156
Self-Esteem - Archangel Michael - 158
Sleep - Archangel Gabriel - 160
Soul Mates - Archangel Chamuel - 162
Space Clearing - Archangels Michael & Raphael - 164
Spiritual Development - Archangel Raziel - 166
Spiritual Path - Archangels Gabriel & Raziel - 168
Study - Archangel Uriel - 170
Tests/Exams - Archangel Zadkiel - 172
Third Eye Opening - Archangel Tzaphkiel - 174
Transformations/Changes - Archangel Azrael - 176
Travel - Archangel Raphael - 178
True to Ourselves - Archangel Michael - 180
Understanding - Archangel Uriel - 182
Wisdom - Archangels Haniel & Uriel - 184
Writing - Archangel Metatron - 186

Abundance
Archangel Raphael

Thank you Archangel Raphael for helping me to recognise abundance in its many forms. Thank you also for helping me to feel gratitude for the abundance I already have, and for the abundance that is continually manifesting.

Addictions
Archangel Tzaphkiel

Thank you Archangel Tzaphkiel for helping me to be aware of my addictive thoughts and/or behaviours that are no longer serving me. Thank you for your love and guidance in relation to how I may gently replace these.

Akashic Records
Archangel Metatron

Thank you Archangel Metatron for helping me to access my akashic records, to gain a clearer understanding of my soul's purpose in this lifetime.

All is Well
Archangel Jeremiel

Thank you Archangel Jeremiel for helping me to trust that all is well - even if my current perception suggests otherwise. Thank you for helping me to observe from a higher perspective.

Angelic Reiki
Archangel Metatron

Thank you Archangel Metatron for assisting me on my angelic reiki journey on all levels. Thank you for guiding me in relation to the next steps to take on this special journey, and helping me to trust everything is unfolding as it's meant to be in relation to divine timing.

Animal Kingdom
Archangel Ariel

Thank you Archangel Ariel for the love, light and support you share with the animal kingdom. Thank you also for sharing this love and light with pets in their times of need.

Argument Resolution
Archangel Raguel

Thank you Archangel Raguel for arguments being resolved peacefully, and reminding me that opposing opinions can be responded to with compassion.

Beauty in Ourselves
Archangel Haniel

Thank you Archangel Haniel for reminding me that the beauty I see in others is actually a reflection of the beauty in myself.

Career
Archangel Chamuel

Thank you Archangel Chamuel for assisting me to review my career regularly, to clarify what is important to me as I evolve and grow, and for supporting me through any changes I wish to make as a result of this.

Cleansing & Clearing
Archangel Michael

Thank you Archangel Michael for helping to cleanse and clear that which is no longer serving me on all levels, in relation to divine timing and the highest purpose of all.

Communication
Archangel Gabriel

Thank you Archangel Gabriel for helping me to communicate authentically and eloquently. Thank you for reminding me of the inner courage and strength I have to speak my truth, and to respond with an honest 'yes' and an honest 'no' when relevant.

Compassion
Archangel Zadkiel

Thank you Archangel Zadkiel for helping me to respond with compassion - especially in situations where my initial response would have previously been of a lower vibration.

Conception/Pregnancy/Birth
Archangel Gabriel

Thank you Archangel Gabriel for sharing your love and light in relation to all matters concerning conception, pregnancy and birth. Thank you for higher perspectives being gained throughout this process.

Cord Cutting
Archangel Michael

Thank you Archangel Michael for helping me cut cords of attachment to that which no longer serves me, and for the energy of those cords being transmuted into mother earth. Thank you also for my awareness of the positive effects this creates.

Courage
Archangel Michael

Thank you Archangel Michael for reminding me of the inner courage, strength, and power I have, and my ability to respond to challenges with grace, love and compassion.

Creativity
Archangel Gabriel

Thank you Archangel Gabriel for helping me to recognise how creative I am, and for finding ways of using my creativity for the benefit of myself and others.

Death/Dying/Grieving
Archangel Azrael

Thank you Archangel Azrael for your support in relation to death, dying and grieving. Thank you for helping those who are dying to pass over peacefully, and thank you for supporting those who are left behind. Thank you also for reminding me that the grieving process is not linear, and is always a unique experience.

Decision Making
Archangel Jeremiel

Thank you Archangel Jeremiel for helping me to make the right decision, based on the highest purpose of all. If I need more information before being able to make decisions, thank you for this being presented to me in ways it is easily understood.

Direction
Archangel Michael

Thank you Archangel Michael for helping me to recognise when I am moving in the right direction, and for noticing when I am not. Thank you for reminding me of the tools I have within to stay on track, based on the calling of my soul.

Divine Guidance
Archangel Jeremiel

Thank you Archangel Jeremiel for helping me to be open to receiving divine guidance, and for recognising when this is being received. Thank you also for reminding me that signs are everywhere, and can sometimes be revealed in the most unexpected ways.

Dreams & Visions
Archangel Jeremiel

Thank you Archangel Jeremiel for helping me to remember my dreams if they contain significant messages for me. Thank you also for my ability to understand and interpret my dreams and visions, if they initially appear to make no sense on a conscious level.

Empowerment
Archangel Raguel

Thank you Archangel Raguel for helping me to feel empowered and motivated when my actions will be of benefit to myself and/or others. Thank you also for helping me to take aligned action in relation to this.

Energy Levels
Archangel Michael

Thank you Archangel Michael for helping me pay attention to my energy levels, and to notice when I need to create some time to rest. Thank you for helping me to create balanced energy levels, by paying attention to how I feel, and acting accordingly.

Eyesight
Archangel Raphael

Thank you Archangel Raphael for helping me to pay attention to how my eyes are feeling, and reminding me to take care of my eyes in the appropriate ways, knowing this will in turn benefit my eyesight.

Follow Healing Path
Archangel Raphael

Thank you Archangel Raphael for helping me to follow the right healing path for me - whether this be in relation to assisting me personally, or learning different healing modalities to share with others.

Follow Heart
Archangel Michael

Thank you Archangel Michael for helping me to follow my heart, and for helping me to notice the positive effects of doing so.

Forgiveness
Archangel Zadkiel

Thank you Archangel Zadkiel for assisting me with forgiveness. As it isn't always easy to forgive, thank you for reminding me that forgiveness is the key to setting myself free. Therefore, thank you for helping me to find the ability to forgive, as and when this is appropriate.

Fresh Start
Archangel Raphael

Thank you Archangel Raphael for supporting me in relation to the fresh start I feel guided to make. Thank you for my awareness of this support in many ways, on many levels.

Good Weather
Archangel Uriel

Thank you Archangel Uriel for helping to create good weather conditions, so a positive outcome is experienced.

Grace
Archangel Haniel

Thank you Archangel Haniel for helping me to respond with grace, and also for helping me to recognise grace in others.

Harmony
Archangel Raguel

Thank you Archangel Raguel for helping to create harmony where this is relevant. Thank you for the positive effect of this harmony being recognised, and therefore being replicated again and again.

Healing
Archangel Raphael

Thank you Archangel Raphael for the amazing healing energy you radiate. Thank you for sharing your healing energy whenever there is a request for this. Thank you for those requesting healing, being unattached to a specific outcome, and simply knowing your healing energy will have a positive effect - whether there will be evidence of this or not.

Healing Modality Support
Archangel Raphael

Thank you Archangel Raphael for supporting me with the healing modalities I am drawn to. Thank you for assisting me in all ways in relation to this, and for ensuring I am always drawn to the right teacher or book based on what I would like to learn, and the best ways for this to happen.

Healthy Habits
Archangel Tzaphkiel

Thank you Archangel Tzaphkiel for helping me to recognise habits that are good for my health. Thank you for my ability to pursue these habits, and for ensuring I always have the relevant time, space and funds required to do so.

Higher Realm Connection
Archangel Tzaphkiel

Thank you Archangel Tzaphkiel for helping me to connect with the higher realms, and for recognising these connections. Thank you also for helping me to implement the results of these connections when relevant.

Home
Archangel Jophiel

Thank you Archangel Jophiel for my home, and for my ability to create a homely environment for myself and those I share my home with. Thank you for my home being a reflection of what is important to me.

Inner Guidance
Archangel Jophiel

Thank you Archangel Jophiel for helping me to trust my inner guidance. Thank you for the courage to take aligned action in accordance with this, in relation to the highest purpose of all.

Intellect
Archangel Uriel

Thank you Archangel Uriel for helping me to use my intellect to understand things objectively, and therefore being able to make decisions taking this into consideration.

Intuition
Archangels Jeremiel & Tzaphkiel

Thank you Archangels Jeremiel and Tzaphkiel for helping me to trust my intuition, and allowing this to guide me - opposed to just conscious reasoning.

Intuitive Skills
Archangel Haniel

Thank you Archangel Haniel for helping me to recognise and implement my intuitive skills, and for my awareness of the positive effects of doing so.

Kindness
Archangel Zadkiel

Thank you Archangel Zadkiel for helping me to embody kindness, and for recognising and responding to kindness in others.

Knowledge
Archangel Uriel

Thank you Archangel Uriel for my ability to recognise the knowledge I already have, knowing this exists in many forms. When I am seeking more knowledge, thank you for assisting me with this to help me evolve and grow.

Law of Attraction
Archangel Jophiel

Thank you Archangel Jophiel for reminding me that every word I speak and every thought I think is creating my reality. Thank you also for reminding me that I attract in alignment with my vibration, so to be more aware of how I am feeling in any given moment.

Letting Go
Archangel Michael

Thank you Archangel Michael for helping me to recognise what no longer resonates with me, and to lovingly release this in relation to divine timing and the highest purpose of all. Thank you also for reminding me this creates space for what resonates with me now.

Life Purpose
Archangel Chamuel

100

Thank you Archangel Chamuel for helping me to remember that my life purpose is based around what I love, and what comes naturally to me. Thank you for reminding me this isn't necessarily about a title or label, but more about the frequency I emit when I am my true, authentic self.

Life Review
Archangel Jeremiel

Thank you Archangel Jeremiel for reminding me to review my life regularly, so I can clarify what I would love to do and be more of, and what I might like to lovingly release. Thank you for these decisions being based on what is truly right for me - opposed to the opinions of others.

Loss
Archangel Azrael

Thank you Archangel Azrael for supporting me through loss, and reminding me to be gentle with myself whilst I work through my own unique process.

Lost Items
Archangel Chamuel

Thank you Archangel Chamuel for reminding me you can help with lost items. Thank you for the trust I have that lost items will be found if and when they are meant to be.

Love
Archangel Chamuel

Thank you Archangel Chamuel for helping me to align with the frequency of love. Thank you for helping me to be loving, and to recognise when I am loved.

Loving Relationships
Archangel Chamuel

Thank you Archangel Chamuel for my significant relationships being based on love. Thank you for my ability to recognise others who's priority and essence is also love.

Manifestation
Archangels Ariel & Raziel

Thank you Archangels Ariel and Raziel for helping me to remember I am always manifesting - whether I am consciously aware of this or not. Therefore, thank you for my awareness of how I am feeling and what I am thinking, and my ability to shift to better feeling thoughts, knowing these lead to better feeling manifestations.

Manifesting Desires
Archangel Jophiel

Thank you Archangel Jophiel for helping me to manifest my desires, by reminding me of the importance of feeling the positive effects of these desires, as if they have already manifested. Thank you for reminding me that each desire (or something better) is manifesting for me, based on the vibration of how I am feeling.

Mediation
Archangel Raguel

Thank you Archangel Raguel for assisting with creating interventions in disputes, in order to gain resolution. Thank you for the higher perspectives gained upon resolution.

Meditation
Archangel Tzaphkiel

Thank you Archangel Tzaphkiel for my ability to recognise the benefits of meditation, and for my awareness of the perfect style for me. Thank you also for helping me to create some time out for myself to meditate, and for noticing the positive effects of doing so.

Memory Function/Recall
Archangel Zadkiel

Thank you Archangel Zadkiel for my ability to absorb, process and store the information I receive. Thank you also for my ability to easily recall information when this is relevant.

Moon Energies
Archangel Haniel

Thank you Archangel Haniel for my awareness of the different phases of the moon, and how these energies can be utilised for the benefit of myself and others in creative ways.

Motivation
Archangel Michael

Thank you Archangel Michael for helping me to be motivated, by focussing my awareness on the positive effects of having taking the action I am feeling guided to take. Thank you for the clarification in relation to what taking the relevant action will enable me or others to be, do or have.

Music
Archangel Sandalphon

Thank you Archangel Sandalphon for helping me to recognise the power of music, and for having an awareness of how different types of music make me feel. Thank you for me being mindful of the music I listen to, and the effect this has on me.

Natural Disasters
Archangel Uriel

Thank you Archangel Uriel for your support in relation to natural disasters. Thank you for ensuring relevant resources are available, and received by those in need. Thank you for the unity that is created as a result of such disasters.

Nature
Archangel Ariel

Thank you Archangel Ariel for reminding me of the importance of being in nature, and the positive effects this creates. Thank you for my appreciation of the natural world, and the gifts this provides for free.

Negative Thoughts
Archangel Tzaphkiel

Thank you Archangel Tzaphkiel for helping me to recognise when I am having negative thoughts, and my awareness of how this affects me physically. Thank you for helping me to gently shift these thoughts to more positive ones, and for then noticing how I start to feel better as a result of doing so.

Parenting
Archangel Gabriel

Thank you Archangel Gabriel for your assistance in relation to parenting. When I could benefit from advice, thank you for directing me to the relevant person - whether this be a family member, friend or professional. Thank you for reminding me I am always doing the best I can, with the resources I currently have.

Patience
Archangel Jophiel

Thank you Archangel Jophiel for helping me to embody patience, when this will be of benefit to myself and others. Thank you for my ability to recognise the benefits of trusting divine timing, and allowing natural flow.

Peace
Archangel Uriel

Thank you Archangel Uriel for helping me to clarify what peace means to me, and for the ways I experience this. Thank you also for the part you play in bringing peace to the world - and beyond.

Persistence with Pursuits
Archangel Jophiel

Thank you Archangel Jophiel for helping me to be persistent with my pursuits - especially when I experience difficulties or challenges. Thank you for helping me to align with the results I wish to achieve, as motivation to continue.

Positive Thoughts
Archangel Jophiel

Thank you Archangel Jophiel for helping me to be consciously aware of the positive effects of my positive thoughts. Thank you also for helping me to search for better feeling thoughts, when I become aware of the thoughts I am having not feeling so good.

Practical Solutions
Archangel Uriel

Thank you Archangel Uriel for helping me to find practical solutions to problems or challenges. Thank you for providing me with inspiration in relation to who to reach out to who could be of help, and for reminding me I don't have to attempt to solve all problems on my own.

Prayer Delivery
Archangel Sandalphon

Thank you Archangel Sandalphon for ensuring my prayers are received, and for helping me to trust this - even if I am unable to obtain physical evidence of this being so.

Problem Solving
Archangels Metatron & Uriel

148

Thank you Archangels Metatron and Uriel for helping problems to be solved in all ways, on all levels. Thank you for my ability to find and implement solutions.

Protection
Archangel Michael

Thank you Archangel Michael for your protection in all ways, on all levels. Thank you also for my awareness in taking responsibility for my own protection, and trusting my intuition in relation to my own safety.

Psychic Abilities
Archangels Haniel & Raziel

Thank you Archangels Haniel and Raziel for helping me to trust my psychic abilities, and for assisting me with developing these if I wish to do so.

Record Keeping
Archangel Metatron

Thank you Archangel Metatron for helping me to keep records and/or accounts accurately. Thank you for these being stored securely, and easily accessed and amended when relevant.

Rest
Archangel Gabriel

Thank you Archangel Gabriel for my understanding of the importance of rest, and for being able to create the time to do so. Thank you for the evidence I receive, that the rest I take is being of benefit to me.

Self-Esteem
Archangel Michael

Thank you Archangel Michael for helping me with my self-esteem and to value myself, by enhancing my ability to recognise my unique skills, talents and worth.

Sleep
Archangel Gabriel

Thank you Archangel Gabriel for helping me to create a tranquil place to enhance my sleep. Thank you for my ability to sleep well, and to notice the positive effects of doing so.

Soul Mates
Archangel Chamuel

Thank you Archangel Chamuel for helping me to recognise a true soul mate connection. Thank you for my depth of understanding in relation to the soul contracts we agreed to, for helping each other to evolve in this lifetime - and beyond.

Space Clearing
Archangels Michael & Raphael

Thank you Archangels Michael and Raphael for helping me with space clearing, so the flow of energy is harmonised and balanced. Thank you for reminding me to space clear regularly, and for my ability to recognise the positive effects of doing so.

Spiritual Development
Archangel Raziel

Thank you Archangel Raziel for helping me to clarify what spiritual development means to me. Thank you for assisting with my spiritual development, and helping me to come to my own conclusions about the meaning and purpose of my life, and my own innate spirituality.

Spiritual Path
Archangels Gabriel & Raziel

Thank you Archangels Gabriel and Raziel for assisting and supporting me on my spiritual path. Thank you for my ability to embody love, kindness and compassion - which in turn benefits all.

Study
Archangel Uriel

Thank you Archangel Uriel for your assistance when I study. Thank you for helping me to create the perfect environment to do so, and for helping me to access the relevant resources. Thank you also for my ability to create the time I need to study.

Tests/Exams
Archangel Zadkiel

Thank you Archangel Zadkiel for helping me with tests and exams. Thank you for my ability to easily recall the information I need, to demonstrate my knowledge, awareness and competence.

Third Eye Opening
Archangel Tzaphkiel

Thank you Archangel Tzaphkiel for assisting with opening my third eye, so I can easily access higher wisdom, insight and intuition, whilst also gaining a deeper spiritual connection.

Transformations/Changes
Archangel Azrael

Thank you Archangel Azrael for supporting me as I experience changes - whether I have initiated these changes myself or not. Thank you also for supporting others who are affected by these changes.

Travel
Archangel Raphael

Thank you Archangel Raphael for your assistance with travel. Thank you for ensuring the journey is relaxing, and that everything runs smoothly.

True to Ourselves
Archangel Michael

Thank you Archangel Michael for helping me to be true to myself. Thank you for my ability to be authentic - without attachment to how others will respond. Thank you also for helping me to take aligned action in relation to what truly resonates with me at soul level.

Understanding
Archangel Uriel

Thank you Archangel Uriel for my depth of understanding, my awareness of others feelings, and my ability to act accordingly.

Wisdom
Archangels Haniel & Uriel

Thank you Archangels Haniel and Uriel for my ability to recognise the wisdom I have gained, and my ability to implement this when and where necessary.

Writing
Archangel Metatron

Thank you Archangel Metatron for assisting with my writing. Thank you for reminding me I have the ability to easily translate what is in my mind into written words, with ease and flow.

About the author

Jo Dance is an Angelic Reiki Master Teacher
and a Meditation Teacher.

Her passion is helping people to
connect with angels in a simple way,
for the benefit of themselves and others.

She delivers live online:
Angelic Reiki Training
Angelic Reiki Sessions
Angel Workshops
Angel Meditation Groups

To find out more you can visit her website:
www.jodance.co.uk

Printed in Great Britain
by Amazon